How To Save $1000 in Just 30 Days

Just 30 Days

Step by Step Guide on How to Save Money & Best Money Saving Tips That Actually Works

ARX Reads

Table of Contents

INTRODUCTION

Today, we're starting your money-saving journey, that's right, whether you're a beginner and you aren't that great at saving, or you're advanced, and you've been doing this a while, these tips are gonna be all about how you can save more of your money, and I'm even gonna show you how you can save $1,000 in just 30 days.

1.Start Your Goal Now!

Start immediately and reverse engineer your goal. We know we want $1,000 in a month. Why $1,000? Great question. Well, it's always great to have a very specific goal. We need to reverse engineer some things, we can understand how we get to any number that you might choose to save.

Not to mention, there was a study done by Statista that said that way too many Americans have very little savings.

In fact, 69% have below $1,000 saved. So, what we're going to do is divide that over that time $1,000 divided by 30 days. This works out to being $33.33

per day, could sound like a lot to some people, could sound like totally achievable for some people, let's break it down.

Let's say you're somebody who likes to go pick up their coffee and definitely likes to go pick up their lunch and might have a little bit of extra cash in their wallet. If you were to omit your $6 Starbucks, your $13 lunch, and add about $14.33, you've got $33.33 per day.

You may not be somebody who goes out to eat all the time, but this is just showing you all the different ways that we can come up with that money. When you give yourself the goal, when you give yourself the baby step, it's a lot easier for you to focus on how to make that goal happen.

However, I have a feeling if you're reading this book, it's not necessarily that you don't know ways to save.

It's more of the issue of the habit of saving, not necessarily being in your life right now.

Because let's be honest, not spending does not always equal saving. Accessible money is very easily spent, if not today, then maybe tomorrow.

So as we're trying to get into the habit of saving, it's very important that not only do we know what our goal is on a monthly, on a weekly, on a daily basis, and now you have that number in mind, we also need to go to step two.

2.Give Your Savings a Home

For this part of the book, I'm so excited to be working with our friends at NerdWallet again, because they have amazing resources for this. NerdWallet does so much, but they're really gonna help us out here because they help you shop for the very best options when it comes to a savings account. They wanna make sure you're earning what you deserve on your savings, and they've researched dozens of financial institutions with the very best options. If we're really going to make our money work for us, as we get into the habit of saving, we want something that is highest in yield with the lowest minimum balance, and that is why I go straight to NerdWallet to find the best options for me out there 'cause it changes and they do all of that work for you.

The NerdWallet app is not only going to help you make sure that you've got a home base for your savings that's going to pay you back the most, but it's also a great one-stop-shop for all of your financial needs.

If you want to easily explore your best financial options, check out NerdWallet.com so that you can download the app for yourself.

3.Make Finance Tracking A Daily Ritual

Step number three is to make it a daily ritual of paying attention to your accounts. This is something that I actually used to make fun of my little brothers for. They're 10 years younger than me, and they were way better than me at this. They would always report to me how much money they had in the bank. I was like, first of all, I feel like that's none of my business, but second of all, their obsessive compulsiveness over it like, literally they would spend $5 so that they could make it like an even $5,000 in the account, it just was prettier for them to look at.

That kind of thought process made them be very, very cognizant of how much money they had, how much money they were spending, and it really gave them much better habits when it came to saving or choosing not to spend when the occasions arose.

So, we're actually going to take their round to zero ideas. We're going to round all of your main accounts like your debit card, or any kind of cash account that you use to pay bills or buy things. We're gonna round it down to a zero.

So, let's say in your checking account, you have $532, I'll give you the option here, but if you're adventurous, you could really be done for the day, if you chose to round down to 500, taking the additional 32, and moving it to your savings account. You've got a fresh 500 in your checking, and you have just added a little bump to your savings account. If that's too much for you, that's okay, round down to 530, and move the $2 over to your savings account.

The point is that you use that round-down mentality so that a little bit every day, moves over to your savings account. It's exactly what you choose, but it's giving you a bar, so if you have $539 in the bank, like okay, I'm moving nine bucks over today, just by default, when that money is being moved to a place where it cannot be as easily spent, who is going to remember $9 by tomorrow, probably not very many of us.

So, whether it's daily or weekly, take your account in your checking to zero and use anything over that zero to put in your savings account, probably not wise to round down to 0.00. That's dangerous territory, as some of us have experienced with managing our bank accounts. Do the responsible amount that makes you feel good, not makes you feel uneasy about your financial situation today.

4.Choose Your YTK Rate

YTK stands for "yours to keep". One of the biggest issues that we have in savings culture today is that, we think we can only save whenever we have leftover. We believe that yes, we signed a lease, we owe our landlord money for rent. Yes, you do pay your rent my friends. However, when we think about saving as something we do first that we pay ourselves first, we start to change the way that we live within our means. And then that live within your means advice that everybody gives, that's just so helpful, thanks everybody living within my means we continue to live paycheck to paycheck, because we're not doing something actively for ourselves first. But if you know what your paycheck is, and you know your YTK rate, you know what's left, and that is your means.

If you were to pick up a financial book, whether they call it, yours to keep, whether they call it, pay yourself first, it doesn't matter. They say that when you get your paycheck, you should save at least 10% immediately, take it out of the equation, put it where it's gotta go. You could decide that some of that gets invested, you could decide that some of it goes into savings, but it gets taken out of the equation when we have to then go start paying bills, going to the grocery store, living our lives.

So, now you just have to decide your rate, what is your YTK rate? Is it 10%, is that a little too high for now? Go to seven, maybe go to five, choose what it is. Maybe you decide to do a bit more, I'm somewhere around 17% right now, because each little bit of percentage gets broken up differently into various different savings for me, but for right now, we're just trying to get to $1,000 in 30 days.

So, if you can take 10% of your paycheck, and you only get so many of those, how much is that and put it in that savings account that you now have, how can you break that down in your goal, if you know you're going to get that twice a month, if you have a steady paycheck, how much of that is gonna help you get to that $1,000 in 30 days? Then you can reverse engineer the rest of your daily goals based on what else needs to cover that $1,000.

5.Make the Save

We need to make this a daily ritual for ourselves, so this is what we're going to do to make sure that we hit our goals.

Now, use a piece of paper. I highly recommend using a calculator for this. We've got to get to our $33.33 per day, so we need t find the ways that we did make that happen. Did we skip Starbucks today? That's $6. What about skipping lunch? That's 13 bucks, we talked about after tip, you know. Now let's say you got paid today a little bit of a separate equation here, right? So, let's say that 10% of your paycheck is $150, we got our $150. Now, we're going to divide that over potentially, 15 days, right? 'Cause that's how many days you had to work to make that paycheck, which works out to being $10 per day.

So, you also get to add your payday right here of $10. Now, you're gonna move $150 at once, but I'm showing you in your daily total that you've achieved $10 contributing it to your daily goal.

Now, our daily goal is $33.33 we only have $29 in total, so that means we're gonna have to come up with cash in the amount of $4.33, So that's a total of $33.33, we have hit our daily goal.

We, every day are going to take that $33.33 out of our easily spent account checking and move it to that savings every day.

If you do the round down, maybe that's where you find the $4.33 there's a number of different ways that this can happen, but you need to formally transfer it to your savings every time you can.

There's gonna be a lot of people saying, why would you transfer money every single day that's so exhausting and dumb? Sure, but if you never have money in your savings account, it has to do with not being able to make this lifestyle change for yourself. So, move that money, make the save every day.

If your goal feels really far away, I wanna share this quote with you from Emily Dickinson. "If you take care of the small things, the big things take care of themselves."

Just chip away at your goal, be very intentional with it, and build that habit.

A Giveaway

I have a very special gift for you!

We make smart and easy explainer content on a variety of different subjects. So, because you have shown interest in one of our products, we are giving away our bestselling courses (cost $20) absolutely FREE!

Visit – arxreads.com/gift

We hope you found this book helpful and if you did, we'd love for you to share your thoughts by leaving us a review of this book. If you have any questions you would like to ask you can reach out to us at *hi@arxreads.com* and we'll be sure to get back to you as soon as possible.

Thank   you!

Notes

Made in the USA
Monee, IL
28 May 2022

97169514R00015